5 SECONDS OF SUMMER

She Looks So Perfect

Mary Boone

TRIUMPH
BOOKS

This book is available in quantity at special discounts for your group or organization. For further information, contact:

Triumph Books LLC
814 North Franklin Street
Chicago, Illinois 60610
(312) 337–0747
www.triumphbooks.com

Printed in U.S.A.

ISBN: 978-1-62937-069-9

Content developed and packaged by Rockett Media, Inc.
Written by Mary Boone
Edited by Bob Baker
Design and page production by Patricia Frey
Cover design by Patricia Frey

Photographs courtesy of Getty Images unless otherwise noted.

This book is not authorized, approved or endorsed by 5 Seconds of Summer. It is not an official publication.

CONTENTS

CHAPTER 1

Back in the Beginning

5 Seconds of Summer may be the best possible evidence that teachers' comments on report cards can make a difference.

Music teacher Adam Day taught Calum Hood, Luke Hemmings and Michael "Mikey" Clifford at Norwest Christian College, in the Sydney, Australia, suburb of Riverstone.

"I started teaching them music in year 7, and they excelled in all the practical activities of music, but were very quiet and shy and reserved – they were very much closet musos," he told the *Sydney Morning Herald* in April 2014.

Day, who played a role in encouraging and mentoring the young musicians, says the three were talented, but they had to be pushed to perform.

"I wrote on their reports back then, that it would be good to seek performance opportunities to develop their confidence," he said.

Despite what appeared to be a serious case of stage fright, the boys – Michael in particular – made no secret of their ambitions.

"Michael always said to me, 'I'm going to be a superstar one day,'" his teacher recalled. "I remember him coming off-stage from a performance one evening and he said, 'Yeah, that's what I'm going to do. I'm going to be famous one day. Watch out.'"

Watch out indeed.

The three Norwest Christian College students joined up with drummer Ashton Irwin and began posting Blink-182, Mayday Parade and Justin Bieber cover songs on YouTube.

Pronunciation Key

For the record, the correct way to pronounce 5 SOS is 5 Sauce. Mispronounce it 5 es-oh-es and you're likely to anger, or at least annoy, the original members of the 5 SOS Fam.

The Urban Dictionary even includes a "5 Sauce" entry along with this tip for correct usage:

New Fan:
Oh my god I've found this amazing new band 5 es-oh-es I love them so much!"

5 SOS Fam Member:
"I will hit you in the throat, were you previously a carrot? It's pronounced 5 Sauce."

Initially, only family and friends watched the videos; recognizing talent, they passed the links on to a larger and larger circle. The video that took off was their acoustic take on Chris Brown and Justin Bieber's "Next 2 You," which has earned 1.5 million views since it was first posted in July 2011.

In November 2011, the manager of Sydney's Annandale Hotel tracked down 5 Seconds of Summer and sent them a message through their Facebook page. Would they be willing to perform at his hipster venue? You bet.

The guys started rehearsing four times a week and writing their own material. "We even practiced in the dark with the lights off," Mikey told Sydney's *Good Weekend*. "I know it sounds weird, but it worked."

Only a couple dozen of 5 SOS's thousands of YouTube fans showed up

Gentlemen and Scholars

5 Seconds of Summer's Luke Hemmings, Michael Clifford and Calum Hood were all students at Norwest Christian College, attending classes by day and uploading covers to YouTube by night. They were normal guys, picking up an occasional gig and even playing before a couple hundred students and their families at the school's Senior Soiree in 2012.

Then everything changed. They picked up drummer Ashton Irwin and replaced their study sessions with studio sessions. Their debut single, "She Looks So Perfect," was released in February 2014 and peaked at No. 1 on the Australian Singles Chart, New Zealand Singles Chart, Irish Singles Chart and the UK Singles Chart. And, their first concert tour of Australia sold out in mere minutes.

Music teacher Adam Day, who taught Calum, Luke and Mikey at Norwest Christian, says the difference between their last school performance and what he saw on stage just a few months later was astonishing.

"I was stunned when they came on stage in Sydney," said Day, who played a big role in encouraging and mentoring the young musicians. "They were just different boys with thousands of screaming girls in front of them."

Day says Norwest Christian isn't exactly an incubator for budding rock stars, but the school does pride itself on its supportive and creative environment. The private school, located in the Sydney, Australia, suburb of Riverstone, provides a Christian education to students from Pre-School to Year 12. Norwest Christian's website boasts that, "the Arts play an important part in the life of the college and the development of each of our students as well-rounded individuals." The school, which has annual tuition and fees of approximately $7,000, has a mission statement that reads: "Excellence in education, Christianity in action."

Day, who now teaches at a private college in Taree, Australia, says that while he is rooting for the guys' success, he is confident they won't let fame go to their heads.

"At school we tried to teach them a lot of values," he told the *Sydney Morning Herald* in March 2013, "and I really hope they can remember them and are able to keep a good life balance."

Using only Facebook and Twitter to promote the release, *Unplugged* reached number 3 on the iTunes chart in Australia and Top 20 in both New Zealand and Sweden.

to that first show, but the guys were undaunted.

They kept singing and posting songs, some more notable than others. One song, though, gets credit for launching 5 SOS into the spotlight. In May 2012, the guys posted a live version of an original song called "Gotta Get Out." Seated on a leather sofa and a couple of wooden stools, they sang:

"And if the earth ends up crumbling down to its knees baby

We just gotta get out

We just gotta get out

Gotta get, gotta get, gotta get out

And if the skyscrapers tumble down and crash around baby

We just gotta get out

We just gotta get out"

Nearly 2.8 million people have seen that music video, but only one of them really mattered. One Direction star Louis Tomlinson tweeted a YouTube link to the track along with the message "Been a fan of this band for a while, everyone get behind them." Many of Tomlinson's 16.5 million followers saw the tweet and checked out 5 SOS. It was love at first listen.

By June 2012, when they booked their first tour – to the Australian cities of Sydney, Melbourne and Brisbane – 5 SOS was selling out 500-seat venues and screaming fans were standing outside those theatres for hours, hoping for a glimpse of this hot, new band. That level of success was enough to help the guys get offers from several major record labels and music publishers.

5 Seconds of Summer signed a publishing deal with Sony ATV Music Publishing and released their first EP, *Unplugged*, in June 2012. Using only Facebook and Twitter to promote the release, *Unplugged* reached number 3 on the iTunes chart in Australia and Top 20 in both New Zealand and Sweden.

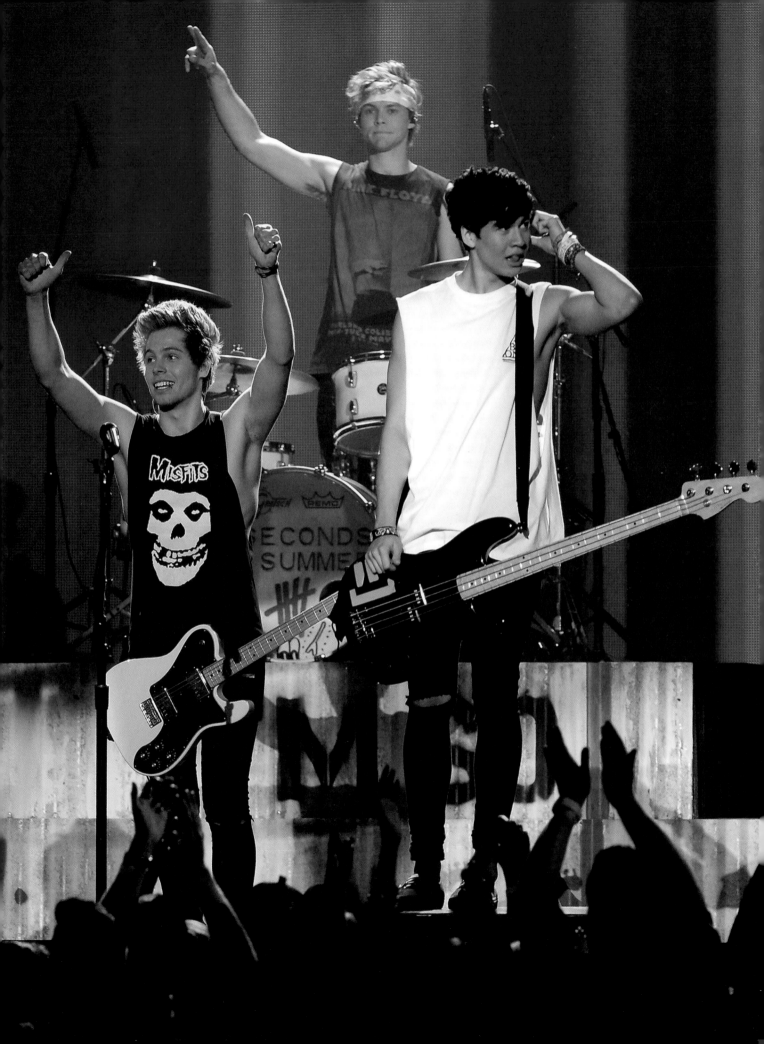

At a Glance

5 Seconds of Summer vs. One Direction

It's easy to see why music critics and industry insiders keep comparing 5 SOS to One Direction. After all, they're both represented by Modest! Management, they came from abroad to take over the U.S. music scene and 5 Seconds opened for One Direction on the latter's 2013 *Take Me Home* world tour.

But, what are the similarities – or differences – beyond that? We offer this quick comparison of the two groups:

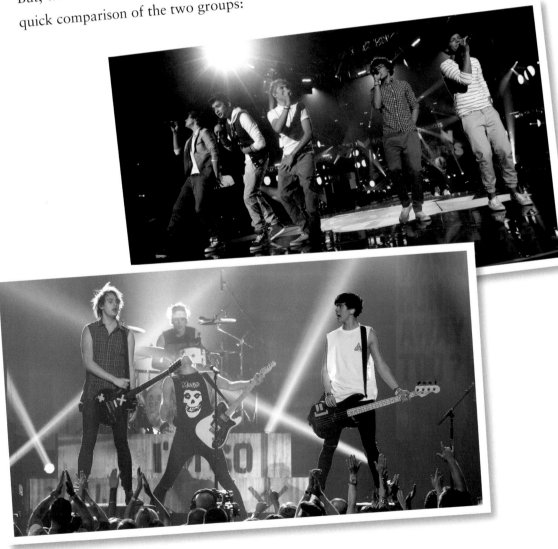

	5 Seconds of Summer	One Direction
The guys	Luke Hemmings, Michael "Mikey" Clifford, Calum Hood and Ashton Irwin	Niall Horan, Zayn Malik, Liam Payne, Harry Styles and Louis Tomlinson
Years active	2011-present	2010-present
Musical style	Punk, rock	Pop, rock
Career boost	Their fan base increased significantly when 1D's Louis Tomlinson posted the link to the YouTube video of their song "Gotta Get Out," saying he'd been a fan of 5 SOS "for awhile." 5 Seconds of Summer's profile was heightened again when, after the release of their first single, "Out of My Limit," Niall Horan tweeting the link to the video clip.	In 2010, the guys auditioned as individuals for *The X Factor* but didn't make the cut. Judge Nicole Scherzinger suggested they compete as a group and the guys agreed. They finished in third place on the reality TV competition, but turned out to be the winners when it came to success. In March 2012 they became the first UK group ever to debut at No. 1 on the U.S. Billboard 200 album chart.
Biggest influences	Blink-182, All Time Low, Green Day, Mayday Parade, Boys Like Girls, Busted	Take That, Bruno Mars, Justin Timberlake
First U.S. TV appearance	*Billboard Music Awards*, May 2014	*The Today Show*, March 2012
First U.S. single	"She Looks So Perfect," 2014	"What Makes You Beautiful," 2012
Setting records	When "She Looks So Perfect" was released in the UK in March 2014, 5 SOS became only the fourth Australian band in history to have a UK No. 1 single, and the first to do so in 14 years.	One Direction's first studio album, *Up All Night* became the UK's fastest-selling debut album of 2011 and topped the charts in sixteen countries; 1D became the first British group in U.S. chart history to enter at No. 1 with their debut album. The group's subsequent albums have also topped the U.S. and UK charts, making them the first group to debut at No. 1 on the Billboard 200 with its first three albums.
Biggest flirt	Ashton Irwin	Harry Styles
Trademark hair style	Messy; looks like they slathered gel on their hands, ran their hands through their hair and called it good. Also oftentimes colorful, Mikey is known for his blue, pink or reserve skunk 'dos.	A little messy; looks windswept even when there's no wind.
Fashion statement	Lots of black denim and leather, skinny jeans, graphic tees, and flannel shirts with the sleeves cut off.	School-boy prep, often color-coordinated among the bandmates.
Body art?	Preference for piercings.	Preference for tattoos, lots of them.
Homeland	Australia – Sydney, to be exact	Niall is from Ireland, the rest of the guys are from the UK
Fans	5 SOS Fam	Directioners
Strum? Drum?	Yes, Luke and Michael play the guitar, Calum plays the bass guitar and Ashton plays the drums.	Not so much. Niall strums a bit and you'll see some air drumming, but that's it for these guys.
Do they have "boy band" dance moves?	No. "We didn't really realize we were a boy band until people started calling us a boy band," Ashton told *USA Today*. "I understand and we don't care what people call us, as long as we're making the music we love."	Not so much. Liam has said: "We just kind of came out and said, 'We can't dance. We're a bit lazy. We're just normal lads.' We look stupid dancing. That's what I think."

The guys got even more 1D love in November 2012, when One Direction's Niall Horan jumped onto the 5 Seconds of Summer bandwagon. Horan, with 18.7 million followers, took to Twitter to share a link to 5 SOS's "Out of My Limit." "Just been showed this video – TUNNNEEEEE!" he tweeted.

Boosted again by social media, the guys quickly got to work songwriting and refining their sound under the tutelage of Christian LoRusso and Joel Chapman of the Australian band Amy Meredith. Chapman even produced the band's EP, *Somewhere New*, released in December 2012.

That same month, the boys headed out on a songwriting trip to London, where they collaborated with artists including McFly, Roy Stride of Scouting for Girls, Nick Hodgson of

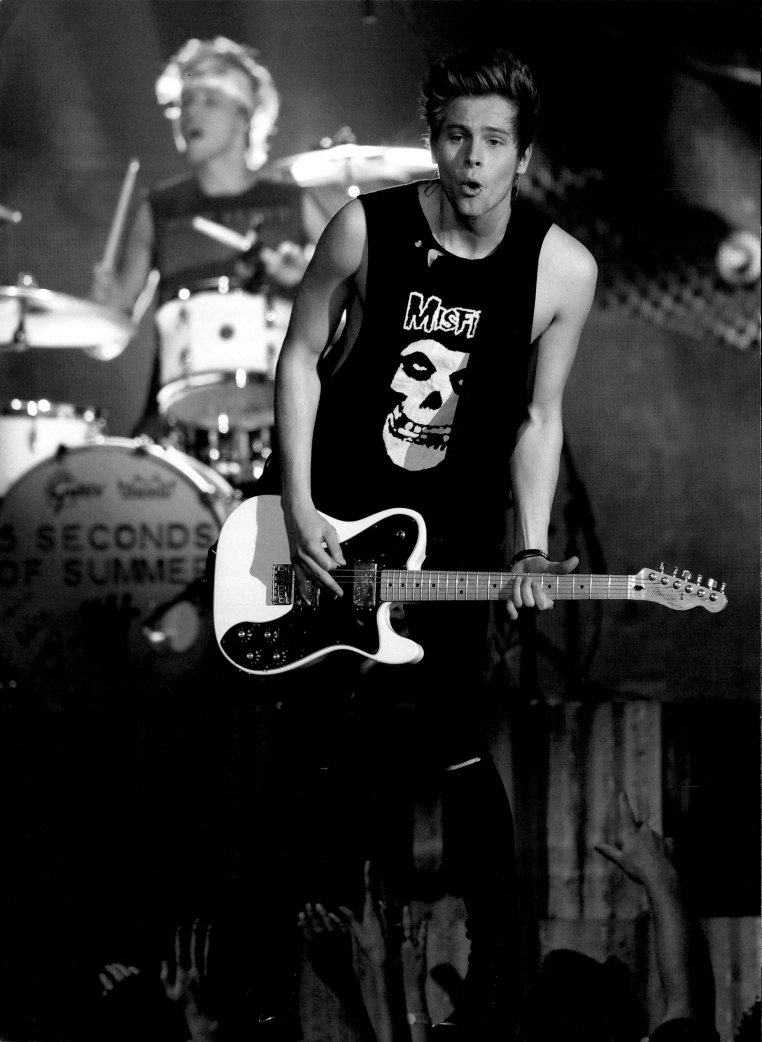

Kaiser Chiefs, Jamie Scott, Jake Gosling, Steve Robson and James Bourne of Busted.

Twitter mentions may have helped jumpstart their careers, but nothing could have prepared them for the super jolt that came in February 2013, when it was announced that 5 Seconds of Summer would open for One Direction on their worldwide *Take Me Home* tour.

Talking with *The Sun*, Luke said he and the guys were initially hesitant about teaming up with 1D. "We looked up to the likes of Blink-182 and Green Day, so we felt that it would be kind of weird for us and we didn't know what to do," he said. "We thought they were cool, but we did look at them as a pop band and we didn't want to be that. But then we met the guys and thought they were awesome."

5 SOS went on to support 1D on the UK, USA, Australia and New Zealand legs of their 2013 tour. "Our first show with 1D was pretty special," Ashton told *The Sun*. "We had to take it from garage playing to arena playing – it was crazy!"

Fun with the Fam

The 5 SOS guys have said that their fans are more like family, so their fans call themselves, "the 5 SOS Fam." The relationship between the guys and their "fam" is light-hearted; fans are included in the major decisions 5 SOS makes regarding their music and image and fans take to social media to poke fun at the guys for being late to everything. Just like a real family.

In November 2013, 5 SOS signed with Capitol Records and immediately began working on their debut album. The lads also signed on as the opening act for One Direction's 2014 *Where We Are* world tour.

As for their old music teacher, Mr. Day? He's not exactly surprised by the guys' newfound fame. They are, after all, skilled musicians – something that sets them apart from stereotypical "boy bands."

"They're highly accomplished in what they're doing, mostly in guitar. They don't just dance in front of a backing track. They're really skilled on their instruments," he said, noting he can't drive anywhere anymore without hearing them on the radio.

Oh, Mr. Day, think of all that airplay as a blessing, not a curse. Those boys took your encouragement to heart and now they're performing on a world stage. What more could a music teacher ask for? ★

CHAPTER 2

International Breakthrough

In 2012, 5 Seconds of Summer was rehearsing in a garage and driving their own cars to small venues around Sydney.

One year later, the band signed to Capitol Records and supported One Direction on the UK, USA, Australia and New Zealand legs of their 2013 tour. They were named MTV Buzzworthy's Fan-Favorite Breakthrough Act of 2013, beating out Haim, A Great Big World, Bastille, Sleeping With Sirens and others.

By 2014, 5 SOS listed its worldwide debut single, "She Looks So Perfect," for pre-order on iTunes and within 48 hours it had reached the No. 1 sales spot in 39 countries.

In January 2014, the guys announced the launch of Hi Or Hey Records, an independent label in partnership with Capitol Records. Two months later, they sold out a 10-date American arena tour in less than five minutes and played a sold-out eight-date headline tour in the

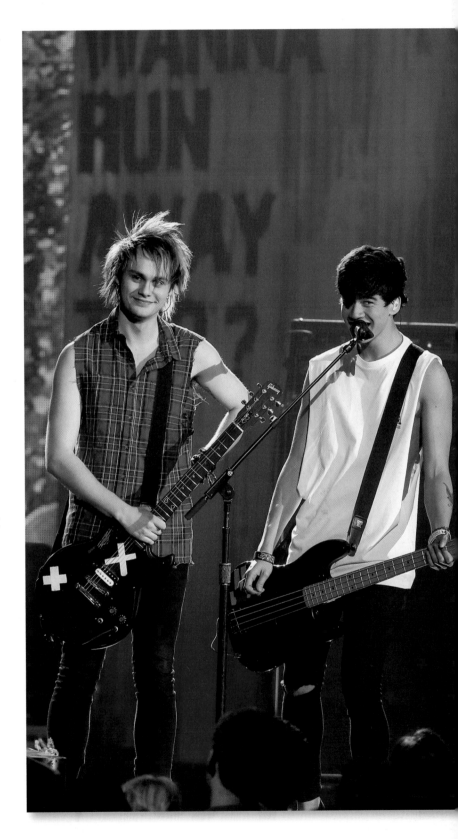

United Kingdom. Then, on March 5, 2014, it was announced that 5 SOS will once again join One Direction on the road, supporting them on their 2014 *Where We Are* tour in the US, Canada, UK and Europe.

Without a doubt, 5 Seconds of Summer have quickly become an overnight international success story. But how did they go from garage band to greatness in such a short time period?

The guys are as baffled as anybody. They say that, until a couple of years ago, they were just another bunch of high school wannabes who "really sucked."

"People hated us," drummer Ashton Irwin told *The Canberra Times* in April 2014. "They told us we were

Praise – and a Few Pans – from Critics

Music critics attend concerts and listen to new albums over and over, often finding fault with the very things fans adore. It's what they do.

Critics' opinions matter because they generally broadcast their thoughts to a broad audience via newspaper, magazine, radio or the Internet.

Here's a sampling of what critics have said about some of 5 Second of Summer's early recordings and performances:

* * *

"This band makes gleaming pop-punk with suburban gloss: no snarl, only lean muscle and blithe cheer. Consider this the next stage of the deconstruction of the modern boy band—from One Direction, a bunch of lads who don't even bother with choreography, to this group, which is, yes, a band and, yes, made up of boys (ages 17 to 19), but not in any way a boy band of old."

—Jon Caramanica reviewing a 5 SOS performance at Best Buy Theatre for *The New York Times*

* * *

"5 Seconds of Summer have been called 'the Australian One Direction' due to their good looks and boyish attitudes, but *She Looks So Perfect* establishes 5 SOS's sound—and it's not pure pop."

—Keely Chisholm reviewing *She Looks So Perfect* EP in *Entertainment Monthly*

* * *

"While this isn't a perfect release, that really isn't the point of this EP. The point is hidden in the underlying potential. These boys have so much coming into their own to do, that with this being their starting point, they are bound to be something great. If this is what they've given us in four songs, we can only imagine what it will sound like when it's 10-12 in a full release, or even a couple of years from now. No, this isn't the next act of the boy band era, but rather the start of a new wave of pop/rock—a wave that was desperately needed in a genre that has been feeling a little stale."

—Victoria Patneaude reviewing *She Looks So Perfect* EP for AlterThePress.com

* * *

"… 5 SOS does an exceptional job at interacting with their fans, and the band does not try to have some fake, squeaky clean image just because they are in front of a lot of people. They have a perfect combo of both fun, upbeat songs to get the crowd pumped up and acoustics."

—Brighid Quinn reviewing a 5 SOS performance in Hershey, Penn., for BlackSquirrelRadio.com

* * *

"It's hard to imagine 5 Seconds Of Summer will ever be seen as a proper rock act, but as long as they're entertaining their very loyal fanbase (as well as hitting No.1 on iTunes in 38 countries), their own brand of punk-pop couldn't feel more alive."

—Lewis Corner reviewing a 5 SOS performance in London for DigitalSpy.com

* * *

"Basically what we love about the lads' new tracks is that they're somehow even bigger and better without being all 'Oh, we need to make music for the masses now.' Hooray."

—Carl Smith reviewing a 5 SOS performance in London for SugarScape.com

bad every single day ... But you have to suck at the beginning and you have to have crap for instruments and not be able to afford stuff and work from the bottom for the band to grow."

"It's been incredible for a rock-pop band like us to come from such a small school in a small town and to be able to do what we do," added Luke Hemmings.

Like Justin Bieber, Austin Mahone, Cody Simpson and others before them, 5 SOS's first fans found them via videos of cover songs they'd posted online. Thanks to kindly Twitter plugs from celebrity fans and One Direction members Louis Tomlinson and Niall Horan, their popularity surged with more than 50 million views on YouTube. Since then, the guys have attracted an enormous social media following of their own; collectively they have amassed 4 million Facebook likes, more than 13 million Twitter followers, and nearly 7 million Instagram followers.

As if making their first U.S. television appearance at the 2014 Billboard Music Awards wasn't huge enough, 5 SOS was actually one of

EP Explained

Ashton Irwin has admitted that a few weeks prior to the release of 5 SOS's *She Looks So Perfect* EP, he actually thought "EP" stood for episode.

In reality, EP stands for extended play. An EP is a recording that contains more music than a single, but not enough music to qualify as a full studio album or LP (long play). The term originally referred to specific types of vinyl records, but it's now applied to mid-length Compact Discs and music downloads as well.

the event's biggest drivers of online conversation. The show's hip and media-savvy audience made 5 Seconds of Summer the most mentioned Twitter account of the evening. The band's official account, @5SOS, was mentioned more than 451,000 times. Along with the personal accounts of its four members, 5 Seconds of Summer as a whole received more mentions than all the other performers and talent at the awards show combined.

But all the social media mentions in the world wouldn't make a difference

Talking the Talk

Fans are hanging on their every word, but sometimes what the 5 SOS guys say doesn't make complete sense. That's because Calum Hood, Luke Hemmings, Michael Clifford and Ashton Irwin tend to use a bit of Aussie slang.

This quick guide to common Australian words and phrases may help your translation efforts:

Ace – Very good.

Barbie – Barbecue, as in *"Throw another shrimp on the Barbie."*

Bities – Biting insects.

Bludger – Lazy person, someone who relies on other people to do things or lend him things.

Blue – A fight, as in *"He was having a blue with that dude."*

Chewie – Chewing gum.

Cozzie – Swim suit.

Dunny (also dunny can) – Toilet, either the room or the specific fixture, especially an outhouse or other outdoor toilets.

Footy – Australian rules football.

Hooroo – Goodbye.

Jumbuck – Sheep.

Lair it up – To behave in a vulgar manner.

Maccas (pronounced "mackers") – McDonald's, as in *"Let's get shakes at fries at Maccas!"*

Pash – A long, passionate kiss.

Ridgy-didge – Original, truthful and genuine.

Spit the dummy – To get upset very suddenly, as in *"He's going to spit the dummy when he finds out his car has been stolen."*

Tucker – Food, nourishment.

Vejjo – A vegetarian.

Yabber – To talk a lot, as in *"Those ladies at the beauty shop sure love to yabber."*

if consumers didn't connect with 5 SOS's look, sound and style. The guys insist they never set out to be the next big boy band – in fact, they absolutely cringe at the label "boy band." They just want to make their own music, their own way.

The guys say their evolution came thanks to perseverance and old-fashioned hard work.

"We did everything," Ashton said. "We rehearsed in the dark! We thought if we can't see what we are doing and we can still play, then we might sound good when the lights are turned on."

Oh, and don't forget cohesion, says Calum Hood, explaining that the 5 SOS guys get along really well, both on and off stage. That camaraderie may be the real secret to their success.

"We're all really good friends," he told *Seventeen* magazine in April 2014.

"I couldn't imagine being in a band with people I didn't like."

These days, even with a record contract, sold-out concerts and their faces on the covers of entertainment magazines, the four pals say they're still wowed by their success – especially when it comes to their popularity with female fans.

"We are still surprised that girls like our band," Ash said, noting that scrawny music kids rarely come out on top of a school's popularity hierarchy. "If you weren't a footballer then you weren't attractive. But it's cool that girls like our band. We're very lucky people want photos with us because one day they won't."

For now, though, the Aussie quartet is hot and getting hotter – as in supernova hot.

Their debut full-length album was released in July 2014, a month selected

Getting Schooled

In the United States, "college" generally refers to a school you attend after you graduate from high school. But in Australia (and Ireland, the UK, Hong Kong and a handful of other nations), "college" may actually refer to a secondary or high school or a school that's affiliated with a university. The 5 SOS guys met while attending Norwest Christian College – but they were only 7th graders.

The guys insist they never set out to be the next big boy band – in fact, they absolutely cringe at the label "boy band." They just want to make their own music, their own way.

for maximum exposure from their summer tour of Europe and North America. The self-titled album features collaborations with John Feldmann (All Time Low, Good Charlotte, Boys Like Girls), Jake Sinclair (Fall Out Boy, Pink), Steve Robson (Busted) and The Madden Brothers (Good Charlotte).

Already in 2014, 5 Seconds of Summer has received six World Music Awards nominations, three MTV Italy award nominations, and one nomination each from *Kerrang!* and MuchMusic. They performed on the finale of Italian TV's *The Voice* and have announced they'll be appearing at Capital's Summertime Ball in London's iconic Wembley Stadium and in New

Who's John Feldmann?

5 Seconds of Summer has collaborated with lots of great musicians to create their debut album, among them John Feldmann. If that names sounds vaguely familiar, it's probably because he's got a pretty impressive musical resume.

Feldmann has produced and co-written songs accounting for sales of more than 34 million albums worldwide. He's also the lead singer and guitarist for the American punk rock band Goldfinger.

Feldman was just 13 when he started playing music; his first band was called Family Crisis.

After touring with a handful of groups, he moved to Los Angeles in 1988 and formed a band called Electric Love Hogs. That's where he met Kelly LeMieux, who later became Goldfinger's bass player.

Feldmann formed Goldfinger in 1994. The group was signed to Mojo/Universal in 1995 and have toured extensively throughout the world. According to his official website, John holds a Guinness world record for performing 385 shows in one year (1996).

Feldmann worked as an A&R (artists and repertoire) rep for Warner Bros. Records and Maverick Records. He's now an A&R rep for Red Blue Records.

Over the years, he's done production work/songwriting for artists and groups including Good Charlotte, The Used, Mandy Moore, Ashlee Simpson, Hilary Duff, All Time Low, Panic! at the Disco, Plain White T's, Boys Like Girls and All Time Low.

5 Seconds of Summer has repeatedly spoken about getting to write and work with Feldmann and All Time Low vocalist and rhythm guitarist Alex Gaskarth, often referring to them as "the dream team."

York City's Rockefeller Plaza for the Toyota Concert Series on NBC's *Today* show.

Despite all that travel and the jetlag that goes with it, Luke, Ashton, Mikey and Calum continue to tweet out love to their fans and take time to sign autographs or post for photos when their schedule allows.

"It's crazy for us, but we're so grateful for every single person who supported us," Calum told *Seventeen*. "Not many people where we live get this kind of opportunity to do what they love." ★

squinting into the teleprompter). Guys, I'm the worst reader. Um… (nervous laughter) They're only getting bigger! Take a look."

The telecast cut to a short video about 5 SOS and then showed a wide view of the stage. Kendall appeared to be saying something, but it was too late because the band's performance was beginning.

Music fans considered the flub an insult to 5 SOS and took their outrage to social media:

> "*Raise your hand if you want to slap Kendall Jenner*" @markoffee tweeted along with a photo of a room full of people with their hands raised.

> "*@KendallJenner I guess all the plastic surgery went to your head*" tweeted @iambizzlex

> "*Kendall Jenner receives the award for being the #1 person the 5sos and 1d fandom hates*" tweeted @stylesharmon

> "*If you ever feel bad about yourself just remember Kendall Jenner almost introduced the wrong band in front of half the world's population*" tweeted @conoremaher

The oldest Jenner sister later took to Twitter to defend herself, saying she left her contacts at home and adding the hash tag #LessonLearned.

Reality TV star and model Kendall Jenner's seemingly innocent mistake made some 5 SOS fans very, very angry.

The teen-age *Keeping Up with the Kardashians* star messed up her introduction of the band at the Billboard Music Awards in May 2014.

Dressed in a cutout white halter top and black sequined pants, Kendall stood on stage and stared into the teleprompter, reading: "The band about to rock the Billboard Awards comes from Down Under, but the direction they are heading is straight up. Recently, they made their debut on the Billboard 200 at No. 2."

Things were going just fine, until she began to trip over her own tongue: "This summer — and now we welcome…one… (long pause,

CHAPTER 3

Luke Hemmings

LUKE

His 5 Seconds of Summer band mates describe Luke Hemmings as "shy," "serious" and "sensible," which makes one wonder about the rest of the guys.

Luke, after all, has freely shared with fans and reporters tales of his tour bus antics – sans clothes.

"When we first got our tour bus in America, I remember in the first half an hour of meeting the tour bus driver, he saw me naked. I thought that was kind of weird," Luke told *RedEye Chicago* in April 2014. "I was running up and down the tour bus without any clothes on and he manages to see me. It was funny."

This sort of off-the-wall behavior is normal for 5 Seconds of Summer. Whether they're wearing party hats to pretend they're unicorns, dancing while wearing chicken masks, attacking each other with fruit or talking to reporters without wearing pants, the guys create fun wherever they go – and even the "shy" one joins in.

Luke Robert Hemmings was born July 16, 1996, in Sydney, Australia. He's extremely close to his parents, Andrew and Liz Hemmings, and his brothers, Ben and Jack. His mom, a math teacher, joined the guys for a bit of their spring 2014 tour and Dad occasionally sends out Twitter messages like: "It's good to have Luke home but boy he is messy" and "Packages delivered to airport. Look out Oz, 5 SOS is on its way. Luke, ya didn't make ur bed when ya left..."

While face-to-face time with his biological family may be limited these days due to tour schedules, Luke and

Luke's Tweets

Luke Hemmings (@Luke5SOS) is a frequent Twitter user, often tweeting six or more times each day. Along with standard promotional fare, he shares video clips, photos and behind-the-scene observations with fans. His comments often focus on travel or food and offer a glimpse of his fun-loving personality:

Just watched John Mayer and now I feel extremely untalented. June 10, 2014

Hotels only serve water with lemon and quite frankly I'm sick of it. June 2, 2014

I live in constant fear of being attacked by an angry banana. June 1, 2014

People with manly jobs hate me. May 22, 2014

Sydney thank you so much, you're incredible. First live TV performance, I was very nervous. We love you x. May 14, 2014

Soup is such an underrated food. May 8, 2014

Imagine if everyone in our band wore loose jeans. May 3, 2014

Sometimes you take a second to see how far you've come from your garage So thankful :-) thank you so much x. April 24, 2014

Just got a milkshake and a hotdog, feeling American. April 21, 2014

My 5sos bracelet is literally stuck on my wrist there's officially no going back. April 14, 2014

I've done more sleeping on planes than in beds this week haha. April 5, 2014

Number 1 in the UK, I think I'm gonna go cry now. Thank you so much! we did it guys xx. March 30, 2014

Watching frozen with the lads. March 9, 2014

Pre show Doritos. Feb. 28, 2014

This house smells like tea and sounds like Usher. Feb. 17, 2014

Scotland I am in your country. Feb. 11, 2014

Calum has a squishy face. Jan. 26, 2014

I got a new guitar today. 😁😁😁😁. Jan. 22, 2014

It's so hard to get my license when I'm never here :-(what's even harder was trying to figure out how to spell license. Dec. 18, 2013

I wanna send a big love to everyone who supports us :-) I think you are all fabulous people x. Dec. 14, 2013

I can't believe we won oz artist :0 love you all x so crazy :-). Dec. 6, 2013

Writing a song with Calum :-). Nov. 22, 2013

his 5 SOS mates say they have become a family of sorts, a real team – with the sum much greater than its parts.

"As a band we are stronger and a proper little family," Luke told *Fuse*. Unfortunately, things haven't always been that way. As kids, Luke, Calum and Michael attended the same private school in Sydney and they've all admitted that they were not friends – not at all.

"Michael didn't like Luke at first, and I was best friends with Michael at the time, so I actually didn't like him,"

Fans are loving 5 SOS's music, whether the songs are about beautiful girls, falling in love with a mannequin or pizza. Of course, the guys' good looks and charm don't hurt either.

recalled Calum in a video the band posted online. "But in the back of my mind I was like, 'He seems like a really cool guy.'"

It's true, confirmed Michael.

"In U9 we hated each other," he said. "He wanted to kill me and I wanted to kill him. And then, somehow, in U10 we became best friends."

As lead singer, Luke is both the band's youngest member and its de facto leader. In a video the band posted online, the guys portray Luke as "smart," "chirpy," "fun" and "happy." They describe him as a teenager with an insatiable appetite ("He'd eat

Love From Liam

One Direction's Liam Payne has said he's "jealous" of 5 Seconds of Summer's musicianship.

"They are so massive now," he told news.com.au in May 2014. "They are … great musicians. I am a bit jealous of them. I am working on learning to play now, but I wish I had put the time in like they did when they were kids," Payne said.

"They are supporting us in Europe and it's huge getting to play stadiums at their age. It couldn't happen to a nicer band."

The Luke Lowdown

Full name:	Luke Robert Hemmings
Birthdate:	July 16, 1996
Astrological sign:	Cancer
Family:	His parents are Andrew Hemmings and Liz Hemmings; Luke has two brothers—Ben and Jack.
5 SOS role:	Lead vocals, guitar
Rep:	Shy, responsible
Favorite food:	Pizza
Favorite singer:	John Ramsay, lead vocalist of the band Marianas Trench
Favorite album:	Blink-182's *Take Off Your Pants and Jacket*
Favorite TV show:	*How I Met Your Mother*
Celebrity crush:	Actress Mila Kunis
Doppelganger:	Actor Jan Uczkowski
On Twitter:	@Luke5SOS
Twitter followers:	2.9 million

Random fact

It's pretty black and white – Luke loves penguins (who doesn't?). He is frequently photographed wearing penguin T-shirts or hats or cuddling stuffed penguins. SugarScape.com has gone so far as to refer to Luke as a "penguin-loving pretty boy."

dinner, then a second dinner, then go to the movie and get a large popcorn and jumbo drink, then he might even go get a snack," they explain.) They say he has a tendency to lose things, but he's also kind and responsible.

"He always chooses the sensible thing to do," said Ashton.

First foes, then friends and now collaborators, Luke and the rest of the guys pride themselves on not only performing great music – but creating it too. Songwriting, they say, is almost always a shared experience. 5 SOS estimate they have written more than 100 songs since they started posting covers on YouTube about two and a half years ago.

"We usually go to write with other people and we'll go in groups of two, so, for instance, Michael and I will go to a songwriting session, and then Calum and Ashton will go to one," Luke explained to *Coup de Main* magazine in May 2014. "We usually come up with an idea to write about or the people that

we're writing with will have an idea, and then we'll try and build a song from that."

It's a formula that's obviously working. Fans are loving 5 SOS's music, whether the songs are about beautiful girls, falling in love with a mannequin or pizza. Of course, the guys' good looks and charm don't hurt either. They sold out every show on their 2014 North America tour and they've managed to earn a lot of press coverage on the release of their self-titled debut album.

Many of those media reports refer to 5 SOS as a boy band, a label that irritates fans because stereotypical "boy band" members don't play their own instruments or write their own songs. The guys themselves seem to take a few deep breaths before responding to such references.

"I think that's going to come with the age we are," he told *RedEye Chicago*. "Obviously we're probably too young to be doing this, I guess. I think we're only going to be called a boy band or not really serious artists (for now). I think after our CD comes out and our EP comes out, people will hear what we do and that we write our own songs and we play our own instruments. I think people will (get it)."

Luke and his band mates are still having a hard time believing their success and good luck. Playing in huge arenas, touring the world with One Direction and performing on internationally televised awards shows is really the stuff of dreams. But no matter how high their songs chart in Asia, or how many fans stand outside a hotel in Mexico just to catch a glimpse of them, Luke says nothing makes him happier than a shout-out from the folks back home in the Sydney suburbs.

In fact, whenever his dad mentions hearing the group's latest singles being played on local radio stations or in shops or businesses near his childhood home, Luke gets all sentimental.

It's "home pride" he told news.com. au. "I reckon people's attitude to us is

Luke and his band mates are still having a hard time believing their success and good luck.

a challenge that motivates us to show them what this band can do," he said.

Challenge accepted, Luke. Your fellow Australians – and the world – think this band can do some pretty amazing things. ★

Music from Down Under

Yes, 5 Seconds of Summer is making a splash with its punk-rock sounds, but Luke Hemmings, Michael Clifford, Calum Hood and Ashton Irwin are hardly the only Australians making music that makes the whole world sing. Here's a quick look at some other Aussies of note:

Iggy Azalea

Amethyst Amelia Kelly – now known as Iggy Azalea – was born in Sydney, but grew up in New South Wales before moving to the United States at age 16. This 24-year-old rapper found UK radio success and supported Beyonce on the Australian leg of her *Mrs. Carter Show* world tour, before hitting it big in the states with her single "Fancy." Her debut album, *The New Classic*, was released in April 2014.

Cody Simpson

Seventeen-year-old Cody Simpson grew up in Gold Coast and found his way to fame via YouTube. He began recording and posting songs during the summer of 2009 and was discovered by Shawn Campbell, a Grammy-nominated record producer who has worked with Jay-Z and other artists. Simpson has toured Europe, doing his own tour dates as well as supporting Justin Bieber on many *Believe* tour dates. During summer 2013, Simpson headlined the *Paradise* tour, featuring opening acts Ryan Beatty and Before You Exit. In fall 2013, he released an acoustic album.

Birds of Tokyo

This five-piece rock band from Perth had a great 2013. Their album, *March Fires*, was certified gold within four weeks of release and the triple platinum single "Lanterns" was the most played song on Australia radio for the first six months of the year. A late 2013 tour with Muse cemented the group's status as one of the country's best homegrown live acts. The alternative rock group is grabbing traction in the United States, where "Lanterns" has enjoyed moderate success.

Vance Joy

James Keogh – better known as Vance Joy – came to music via an unusual pathway. Born in Melbourne, he has an arts/law degree from Monash University and was a semi-professional Australian-rules football player before he started playing open-mike nights. He released his debut EP, *God Loves You When You're Dancing*, in March 2013. His single "Riptide" was voted No. 1 on the 2013 Triple J Hottest 100; the song also became a Top 10 hit on USA's adult-alternative airplay chart. Both Shazam and Spotify have pegged him to make a worldwide splash in 2014.

Boy & Bear

Boy & Bear was formed in 2009 in Sydney, first as a solo project for Dave Hosking, then morphing into a five-piece folk-rock band. The group's 2011 album, *Moonfire*, went platinum in Australia and won five ARIAs (equivalent to a Grammy Award), including album of the year. Boy & Bear's single "Southern Sun" broke into the Top 10 on *USA Today*'s adult-alternative airplay chart.

CHAPTER 4

Micheal
"Mikey"
Clifford

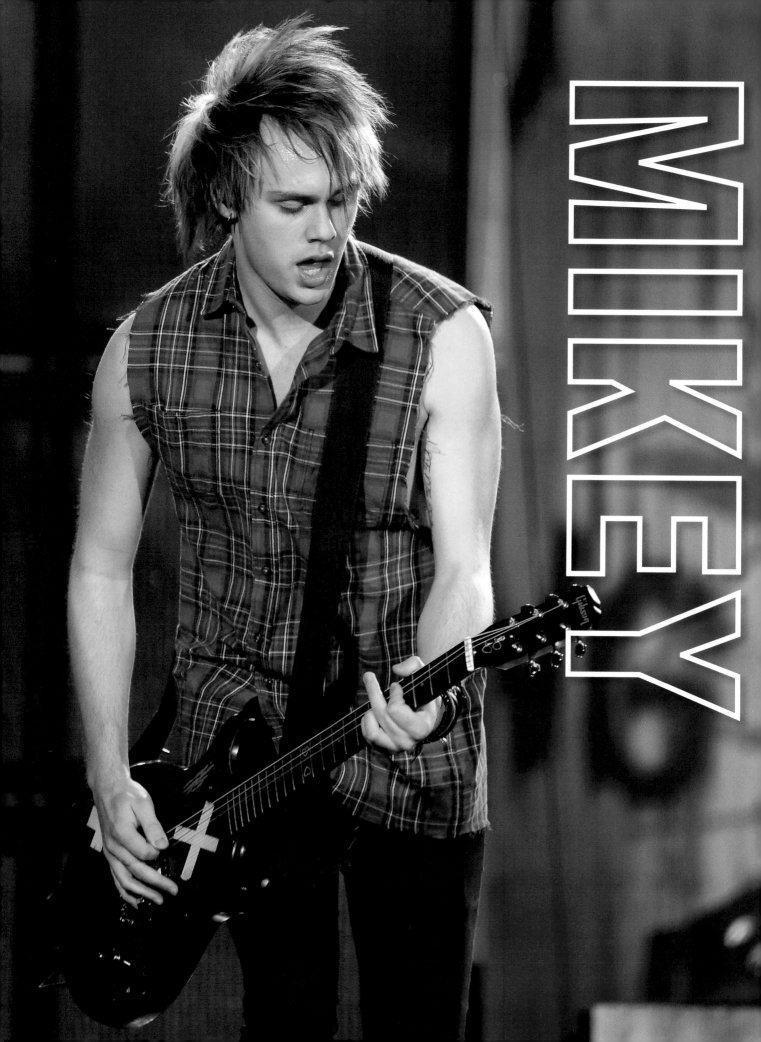

MIKEY

Michael "Mikey" Clifford says the secret to 5 Seconds of Summer's enormous success is simple: hard work.

Sure, talent, good looks and a shout out from 1D's Louis Tomlinson helped, but he insists that without dedication and determination, those things would have gotten them nowhere.

"I think when we started, we were just doing it for fun and, I mean, then eventually we got serious about it and we realized, wow, this could be something. And we just worked our butts off," Michael told the American entertainment TV show *Extra* during a May 2014 interview.

He said during an interview with Singapore Radio that being in a band "means you can have a career with your three best friends." He snapped out of mushy-mode and told the interviewer that if he wasn't making music, "the other boys would probably have jobs and stuff, but I 100 percent would be doing nothing."

"I think when we started, we were just doing it for fun and, I mean, then eventually we got serious about it and we realized, wow, this could be something. And we just worked our butts off."

An only child, Michael Gordon Clifford was born November 20, 1995, in Sydney. His band mates describe him as "weird," "nerdy," "sassy," "sloppy" and "funny."

"He's always there to cheer you up when you're down," Calum said in a series of videos the band posted of themselves in December 2013. "He's just a great friend overall."

Michael attended Norwest Christian College with Calum and Luke, but admits academics were never really his thing.

"I got a D in music," he told the *Daily Mail*.

No, he may not have been known as a scholar, but Michael's hair did – and continues to – get him noticed.

The Michael Lowdown

Full name: Michael Gordon Clifford

Birthdate: November 20, 1995

Astrological sign: Scorpio

Family: Mom is Karen Clifford

5 SOS role: Guitar, vocals

Rep: Wild, sassy

Favorite food: Cheeseburgers – no onion, no pickle

Favorite singer: All Time Low

Favorite album: *The Best of Queen*

Favorite movie: *Forrest Gump*

Celebrity crush: Actress and singer-songwriter Ariana Grande, actress Chloe Moretz, singer Camila Cabello

Doppelganger: Musician Pete Wentz

On Twitter: @Michael5SOS

Twitter followers: 2.6 million

Random fact

Michael says he loves not wearing clothes, a sentiment shared by several of his band mates. Speaking to The Hits, Michael said: "The nakedness gets pretty bad…if you can't be naked what can you be? The words to live by."

"The first time I ever saw a proper fringe was on Michael," said Calum, describing his friend's hairstyle in a band-produced YouTube video. These days, his hair is generally spiked upward with a generous fistful of gel, but more notable than its gravity-defying forces is its constantly changing color. Within the past few years, Michael, a natural blonde, has dyed his locks green, blue, pastel pink, hot pink, purple, white and – for a while – he sported a reverse skunk 'do with white sides and a black stripe down the middle. Countless websites, Facebook pages, Pinterest pages and Tumblr sites are dedicated to tracking the young musician's evolving hairstyles.

While parents may refer to Michael as "the one with the hair," true 5 SOS fans know he's a very talented guitarist. It's a skill he's been refining for some time now.

"Michael used to say to me that he was going to be a rock star one day, which I used to brush off lightly," said Adam Day, the Norwest Christian College music

Within the past few years, Michael, a natural blonde, has dyed his locks green, blue, pastel pink, hot pink, purple, white and – for a while – he sported a reverse skunk 'do with white sides and a black stripe down the middle.

Not That Michael Clifford

Michael Gordon Clifford is first and foremost in the minds of 5 SOS fans. But there are a couple other famous Michael Cliffords worth knowing about.

Michael K. Clifford is an American businessman who is credited with leading the first accredited non-profit university to convert to a for-profit company. He is considered an education entrepreneur and finance strategist.

Michael R. "Rich" Clifford is a former U.S. Army officer and NASA astronaut. He logged more than 12 hours of spacewalk time during three Space Shuttle Missions.

Mikey's Tweets

Michael Clifford joined Twitter in November 2011 and has since shared nearly 9,000 tweets. The sometimes-potty-mouthed guitarist's profile reads: "If you like me, I probably like you more. I play in a band, so do other people in my band." Mikey often uses Twitter to promote shows and songs, to thank fans and to poke fun at his band mates. Here's a sampling:

Can't believe we were just on stage in Wembley Stadium. 😁😁😁😁. June 6, 2014

I want to see the fault in our stars but I don't want to cry ... #firstworldproblems #imasuckerforsadmovies June 5, 2014

If you like our band I probably like you more than Luke does. June 4, 2014

I looked like a wet dog on stage tonight it wouldn't stop raining. May 28, 2014

Just watched a chick flick with Luke, now we need to do something manly like pushups or eat steak. May 27, 2014

We wouldn't have new fans if it weren't for the old ones. May 26, 2014

I forgot to tell u guys I made my hair blonde yesterday. May 17, 2014

Tweeted about jetlag 4 times in 24 hours oops. May 17, 2014

#1 on American iTunes. Holy Balls I love you. May 14, 2014

Happy mother's day mummy :D <3. May 11, 2014

We are performing at the BBMAs. I promise I'm not lying. May 2, 2014

I can't stop eating sour worms. April 15, 2014

Good morning USA I've got a feeling that it's going to be a wonderful day. 🎶 April 8, 2014

Business meeting in 5 mins; still naked in bed with no worries. March 31, 2014

So pumped to be doing more of the stadium tour with the 1D lads!!!! March 21, 2014

All I want is for Luke to game with me. March 5, 2014

Should've brought a coat to our gig tonight. So cold lol. Thank you for having us oxford! Good luck with the dictionary and such x. Feb. 28, 2014

I honestly think @AlexAllTimeLow has the greatest voice of all time. Feb. 20, 2014

Had my first basketball game tonight. Lakers ftw. Jan. 28, 2014

I promise we will have an album this year lol. Jan. 8, 2014

teacher who encouraged the guys to develop their talents. "He's one of those guys who proved me wrong. They were always gifted musicians compared to a lot of the other Year Seven and Year Eight students on the guitar."

Guitar groupies may be interested to know that Michael plays Gibson guitars, largely because that company invited him to visit their London showroom at the start of 5 SOS's United Kingdom tour.

"It was insane, we just walked into this room full of guitars, it was insane," he said. "They let me borrow one and I have been playing them ever

since."

Specifically, he uses two Joan Jett signature Gibsons, as well as a Signature T Les Paul Goldtop and a Slash Signature. Michael says his "first proper guitar" was an Epiphone Les Paul, so the brand holds a special place in his heart.

Fans love to take to social media to chat about all things Mikey – from his mastery of the five-string and his edgy vocals to his hair color and overall good looks. They spread the buzz about 5 SOS so quickly that shortly after they began opening shows on 1D's 2013 *Take Me Home* world tour, they – like One Direction – were getting mobbed every time they left their hotel. Virtually overnight, the 5 SOS lads went from being unrecognized to being unable to go out in public without security.

The guys appreciate that their fans are their best publicists and defenders. For example, when James McMahon, editor of *Kerrang!* magazine, branded the band "rubbish," there was backlash from the 5 SOS Fam around the world. McMahon said he'd just listened to a 5 SOS's Green Day tribute that is slated

House Mates

In mid-June 2014, the 5 Seconds of Summer gents revealed that they've become housemates. The guys spilled the beans while chatting with a reporter from the Australian magazine *Dolly*.

Ashton Irwin, for one, loves the new living situation. "It's the best thing ever," he said. "Living with your three brothers is the best thing you could ask for. There is never a dull moment."

The boys say the house is messy and very, very loud. "It's lucky we all like each other, really," said Michael Clifford.

to be on a compilation *CD Magazine* was producing. He took to Twitter to share his thoughts and later tried to defend his opinion with this follow-up Tweet:

"I did a tweet saying that 5 Seconds Of Summer are rubbish. Because, y'know, I'm a 33 year old man with a beard. Now I am feeling THE WRATH. Here's what I think about 5 SOS as Kerrang! Editor. They are rubbish but if they help somebody get into The Descendants one day, then

AWESOME."

Fans didn't consider that much of an apology and offered a slew of Tweets in rebuttal, many of which included foul language. Here are a few of their more G-rated responses:

@luhluke tweeted @jamesjammcmahon Do i smell jealousy?

@jamesjammcmahon tweeted

Who do you think you are judging people? Ever heard of the phrase if you have nothing nice to say don't say it at all @georgiaaa_horan tweeted @ jamesjammcmahon They've got a lot more fans than you

Michael and the guys know 5 Seconds of Summer wouldn't be touring or recording or enjoying the level of success that they are if it weren't for their ardent supporters. That's why they say thanking their fans is the most important thing they do every day on the road.

"When your whole career is based around other people supporting you, being grateful about everything they have done for you is the most important thing, other than the music," Michael told the *Daily Telegraph*.

Gracious, grateful guitarist. That's Michael Clifford in three words. ★

What's that on Michael's Toast?

There's something smelly coming from the 5 Five Seconds of Summer tour bus. No, the stench isn't coming from the guys themselves, but rather from that dark brown paste they like to spread on their toast.

It's **VEGEMITE**, a food item that's as much a part of Australia's heritage as kangaroos and crocodiles. The 1980s Men at Work single "Down Under" makes mention of Vegemite and the "Happy Little Vegemites" song is sung by Australians young and old.

Vegemite is made from brewer's yeast extract (a by-product of beer manufacturing) and various vegetable and spice additives. It's salty and slightly bitter.

The most common method of eating Vegemite is on toasted bread with one layer of butter or margarine before spreading a thin layer of Vegemite. Other Aussies enjoy their Vegemite sandwiches with cheese, lettuce, avocado or tomato.

It has often been said that Vegemite is to Australians like peanut butter is to Americans. But Vegemite's official company website cautions against trying to eat Vegemite by the spoonful.

"For the optimum Vegemite sandwich you only need a dab," advises the company. "Dip your knife in the Vegemite, and scrape up just a bit – start small if you're a first timer. It will mix right in with the butter and spread easily."

In addition to its use in sandwiches or on toast, Vegemite can be dissolved in boiling water and sipped as a sort of tea, or enjoyed with honey on crackers.

Vegemite is certainly one of Australia's most famous culinary treats, but there are others you should know about:

Lamingtons – This delectable dessert is basically a square piece of sponge cake dipped in chocolate icing and rolled in a sort of dehydrated coconut. Lamingtons are sometimes served as two halves with a layer of strawberry jam or whipped cream. The sweet treat was inducted into the National Trust of Queensland's list of Heritage Icons in 2006; since then each year on July 21, Australians celebrate "National Lamington Day."

Meat Pies – These small pies are filled with ground beef, gravy and covered with a tomato-based sauce. These pies are often eaten as a carry-out item, but can also be served on a bed of mushy peas or mashed potatoes (this is called a "pie floater.")

The Lot – Order your hamburger with "the lot" and you'll be getting, well, A LOT. In Australia your meal starts with a bun and ground beef patty or "mince" as it is commonly referred to there. Onto this foundation, your chef will add lettuce, tomato, onion, cheese, fried egg, sliced pineapple, bacon and a slice of beet root. It all adds up to a sandwich that's hard to wrap your mouth around.

Chiko Roll – This savory snack is sold at football matches, pubs and fish-and-chip shops. The Chiko is basically a super-sized egg roll most often filled with beef, celery, cabbage, barley, carrot, onion, green beans and spices. Developed in the 1950s by caterer Frank McEncroe, the item was originally called a "Chicken Roll" despite not having any chicken in it. It was later renamed the "Chiko Roll."

Potato Cakes – When fish and chips just aren't enough, a side order of potato cakes is sure to please. Also known as potato scallops, these giant circles (4 to 5 inches in diameter) of mashed potatoes are dipped in a batter (like fish batter) and deep fried. They're crispy, tasty and 50 times bigger than a French fry!

Dagwood Dogs – Also known as Pluto Pups, these deep-fried hot dogs are encased in crispy dough. They're close cousins to America's corn dogs, except that Dagwood Dogs are sold pre-dipped in ketchup.

CHAPTER 5

Calum Hood

If it weren't for being pushy, Calum Hood might not be a member of 5 Seconds of Summer.

Michael Clifford and Luke Hemmings were 15-year-old schoolmates when they first decided to start the band. That's when bass guitarist and vocalist Calum says he "somehow wedged my way in."

Thank goodness for assertiveness.

Calum Thomas Hood was born in Sydney on January 25, 1996. While he's often thought to be of Asian descent, he's not; Cal's mother is from New Zealand and his dad is Scottish. His older sister, Mali-Koa, also is a singer-songwriter; she competed on the 2012 season of *The Voice – Australia* under the tutelage of Good Charlotte front man Joel Madden.

Music now seems a natural fit for Calum, but he actually grew up thinking he might become a professional footballer – that's "soccer player" for the Americans in the crowd. The Liverpool fan, who represented Australia and had a promising football career before becoming a full-time rocker, said

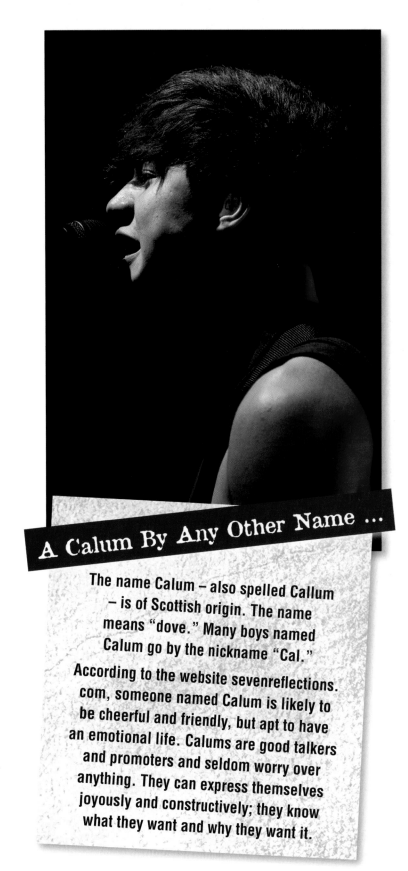

A Calum By Any Other Name ...

The name Calum – also spelled Callum – is of Scottish origin. The name means "dove." Many boys named Calum go by the nickname "Cal."

According to the website sevenreflections.com, someone named Calum is likely to be cheerful and friendly, but apt to have an emotional life. Calums are good talkers and promoters and seldom worry over anything. They can express themselves joyously and constructively; they know what they want and why they want it.

The Calum Lowdown

Full name: Calum Thomas Hood

Birthdate: January 25, 1996

Astrological sign: Aquarius

Family: Mom is Joy, sister is Mali-Koa Hood

5 SOS role: Bassist

Rep: The guys say he's the weirdest person in the band and that he's always up for an adventure.

Favorite food: Pizza

Favorite singer: Australian singer-songwriter Guy Sebastian

Favorite album: Anything by Dragonforce or Nickelback

Favorite TV show: *Family Guy*

Celebrity crush: Singer Katy Perry

Doppelganger: JC Caylen, a guy who's become famous because of the YouTube videos he posts; his YouTube channel has nearly 1.3 million subscribers.

On Twitter: @Calum5SOS

Twitter followers: 2.7 million

Random fact

While opening a 2013 show for One Direction in Melbourne, Australia, Calum's pants split open – from the crotch to the knee. While still playing, he had to slide backstage and have techs duct-tape the seam. "That was kind of hard to do and it was pretty embarrassing," he told *USA Today*, "but I just had to announce it to the crowd to make it less embarrassing."

he still likes the sport but his schedule doesn't allow time for it.

"Every now and then I put the boots back on but for now it's 100 percent focusing on music," he told the *Rouse Hill Times*.

In a series of videos 5 SOS posted in December 2013, Calum's band mates describe him as "the weirdest person in the band" and "like a cuddly little bear."

"He is always relaxed in, like, the most stressful situations," said Luke.

Levity, it appears, is Calum's go-to tool for de-stressing. During an August 2013 interview with Australia's "The Bump" radio program, he admitted that the

In a series of videos 5 SOS posted in December 2013, Calum's band mates describe him as "the weirdest person in the band" and "like a cuddly little bear."

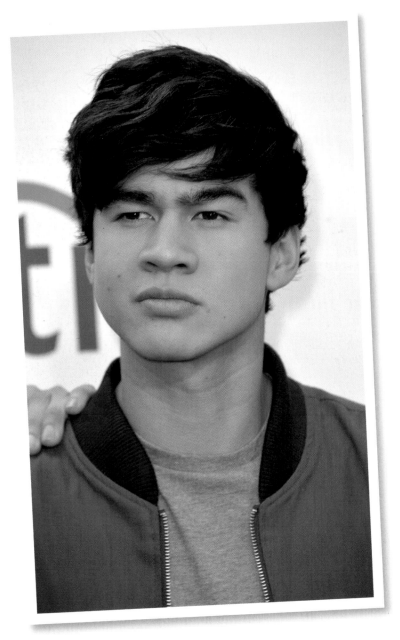

backstage piggy-back races, impromptu wrestling, upside down couch sitting and synchronized dancing that he and his band mates engage in often lead to uncontrollable laughter. The antics have earned the 5 SOS guys a reputation as "troublemakers," something they've tried to keep in check while touring with the equally fun-loving fellows of One Direction.

"There aren't too many pranks (on tour)," Calum told *Seventeen* magazine. "(One Direction) has scary security guards. We avoid the security guards as much as we can. There's usually a lot of fruit throwing though. They're really funny guys. Their humor is really similar to ours."

And the comparisons of the two groups don't stop there:

- "Indeed, (5 Seconds of Summer's) out-of-nowhere success recalls One Direction's stateside takeover in 2012," wrote *Billboard*.
- The blog Jezebel proclaimed 5 SOS is like One Direction "in that they like to joke around a lot and are not from America."

Calum's Tweets

Twitter allows musicians to reach out to fans to create a bond that didn't exist even a decade ago. Bass guitarist Calum Hood first joined Twitter in November 2011; he's since sent out more than 12,500 messages to his 2.6 million followers. Here's a sampling of his rarely serious tweets:

Don't gots much voice. June 7, 2014

Playing on the finale of @THEVOICE_ITALY in a few days! Can't wait! I'm hoping to eat a lot of spaghetti. June 3, 2014

Usual mornings are a text from one of the boys asking if I'm awake and hungry. May 31, 2014

This is wicked. We're on the cover of Rolling Stone Oz! May 28, 2014

I wanna thank every single one of you for supporting this band. God only knows what I'd be without you. May 19, 2014

The first time I'm listening to our album from start to finish. May 1, 2014

Mum got my bed new sheets and they're really girly :(April 28, 2014

Biggest headline show we've ever played tonight!! What a dream to be playing to you Connecticut :) April 25, 2014

Chicago your airport smells like popcorn. April 16, 2014

How do you say we love you in Italian? April 3, 2014

Just found out that we got our very first number one in aus and nz!!! This is the best feeling ever. Thank you thankyou thankyou thankyou xx. March 29, 2014

You look so perfect standing there with my American Apparel teddy bear. March 17, 2014

5 countries in 5 days. March 5, 2014

All Michael and Luke have done tonight is run in my room jump on my bed and leave giggling like little children. Feb. 18, 2014

You guys are the best fans in the world, hands down. No doubt, full stop. Feb. 14, 2014

Siri struggles to understand me. Feb. 3, 2014

So I'm leaving @5sos to start a late 90's Pink cover band after watching her show tonight, plus she's really, really fit. Jan. 29, 2014

This night's a perfect shade of dark blue. Jan. 15, 2014

Best thing about Christmas is FAMILY :) Dec. 24, 2013

No matter how weird my tweets are you guys always go along with it and that is why I love u. Dec. 19, 2013

- Bustle, an entertainment-oriented news site, wrote: "5 Seconds of Summer, better known to the fans as 5 SOS, are known in the United States as that band that kept you entertained before One Directon came on during their *Take Me Home* tour. Or as that band that Louis Tomlinson tweeted about being "a fan of… for a while." Or as that band who will be opening for 1D on the North American leg of their *Where We Are* tour later this year. Or as that band that is practically begging for 1D comparisons for the rest of their career."

These Guys Are Bananas

Call it boredom. The 5 SOS lads have taken to drawing faces on bananas. If they peeled and ate the fruit, the story would end here. But they don't. Luke, Mikey, Calum and Ashton have been making and sharing short videos of their often angry and always animated bananas. The vids are appealing to fans, who have begun holding up "Angry Bananas" at 5 SOS shows.

In early June 2014, the group's fruit fascination made headlines in entertainment publications around the world when they used a banana to face-slap anyone in its path … and One Direction's Niall Horan just happened to be in its path.

What's next? Mango attacks?

Seriously? They're guys. They're in a group. They're not from the United States. And they like to goof around. That's all it takes for critics to label 5 Seconds of Summer "the next One Direction"? Try again. No disrespect to 1D, they're pretty great at what they do, but the two groups have very different sounds and styles. While One Direction's pop has become a little edgier over time, 5 SOS has been known for its guitar-driven anthems right from the start – think Green Day or All Time Low.

The 5 Seconds of Summer lads say there's no sense of competition between them and 1D – a band that actually helped launch their career – and they say that they're honored to be able to tour the world with Harry, Niall, Zayn, Louis and Liam.

"Learning how to tour from the lads really changed our lives," Calum told *Seventeen*.

While performing in front of sold-out arenas and stadiums is a rush, Calum and the rest of the 5 SOS crew admit that there are occasions when they feel a little homesick.

Blather About Briefs

5 Seconds of Summer's breakout single, "She Looks So Perfect," has the whole world singing about underpants:

*You look so perfect standing there
In my American Apparel underwear
And I know now, that I'm so down
Your lipstick stain is a work of art
I got your name tattooed in an arrow heart
And I know now, that I'm so down*

No doubt that it's a snappy chorus about some fairly famous American-made skivvies. But corporate types can sometimes be uptight about rockers singing their brand name over and over, which left lots of folks wondering: "What did the American Apparel big-wigs think of the tune?"

It took a while, but in mid-June 2014, the company finally responded to the song with this official statement: "We're flattered anytime we're mentioned in someone's music or art – especially a big summer anthem like this. Naturally, we also think women look great in our underwear."

Whew. The guys say they've gotten no free underwear out of the deal, but they've also managed to get by with no cease and desist order and no lawsuit. That, 5 SOS, is a victory.

"I always miss my family and friends when I'm on tour, it's just natural," Calum told the (Sydney) *Daily Telegraph* in November 2013. "But when you're playing to 20,000 people each night, doing what you love, it makes it 100 times easier."

It's also got to ease the pain when you find yourself catapulted onto the U.S. Billboard Hot 100 chart, realize your shows are selling out in mere minutes, and get to hobnob on the red carpet with the likes of Katy Perry, Miley Cyrus and Nicki Minaj.

"You always feel a bit of pressure," Calum told *USA Today*. "The boys and I have high expectations of what we want to achieve, but we're really just having fun at the moment and taking it day by day." ★

Hi Or Hey Records

In spring 2014, just as the 5 SOS guys were getting ready to release their debut album, they had another big announcement: The launch of their own record label.

Called "Hi Or Hey Records," it is an independent label established in partnership with Capitol Records. In announcing the project on their website, the guys wrote:

"We have created this label for you guys. We have achieved so much together over the last two years and if it were not for you, we don't know where we would be.

As we get ready to release our debut album, we want to make sure that nothing changes and we keep working together to make all of our dreams become reality. We hear amazing stories from our fans every day of how you spread the 5 SOS word. From our friends in the Philippines who have campaigned to get our songs on the radio for the last 12 months, to the amazing girls in France who postered all around Paris, we are blown away by your support. We love watching you all come together around the world for your 5 SOS meet-ups."

The guys said they plan to release all their music through the Hi Or Hey record label. And eventually they plan to sign their own bands and release them on the label. Their website announcement continued:

"'Hi Or Hey Records' means we can stay in control of our career. Things have gone pretty well with you and us running the show so we want to keep it that way.

We are building a website for the label where you will get to have your say in everything we are up to as well as show us all the incredible things you have been doing to spread the 5 SOS word.'"

The new label's website is www.hiorheyrecords.com

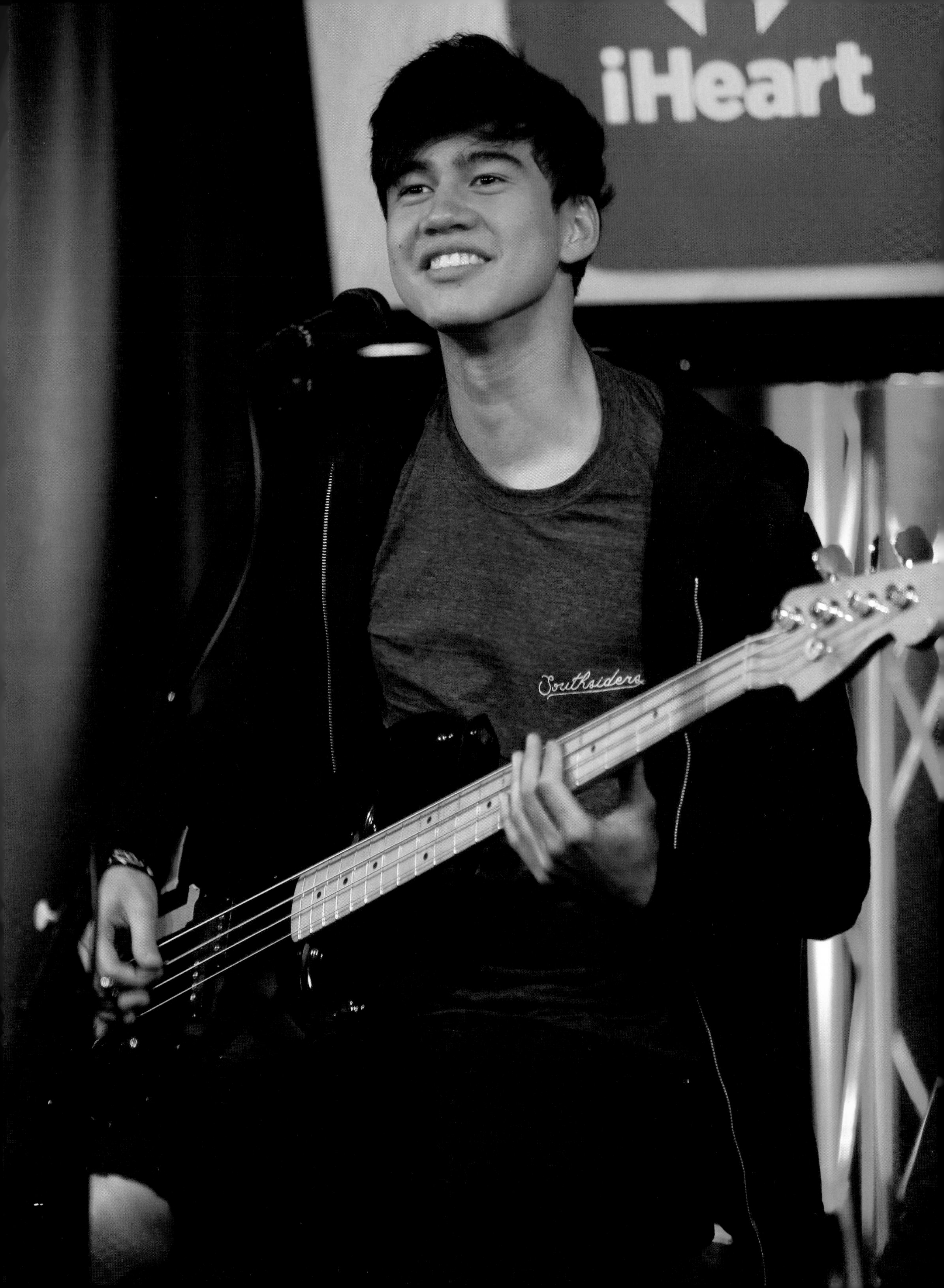
iHeart
Southsiders

CHAPTER 6

Ashton
Irwin

ASHTON

5 Seconds of Summer may be taking the world by storm, but they haven't always been rock stars when it comes to music. In fact, Ashton Irwin told an interviewer on Sydney's *Sunrise* morning television show that he got a big fat "F" in music class at TAFE, a vocational education and training institute.

"I went to TAFE for music and I failed music performance. It was a pretty sad moment really," Ashton said. Perhaps it was the distraction of performing with his new band that kept Ashton from hitting the books and rehearsing for class like he should have.

"We make it sound like we were … we did OK in music … My TAFE teacher inboxed me on Facebook the other day and was a little mad because I hadn't put TAFE in the best light," Ash told Australia's "Kyle and Jackie O" radio show in May 2014.

Now that teachers aren't doing the grading, fans are giving Ashton and his fellow rockers high marks for artistic style, technical accuracy, tonal quality and overall musicianship – A's across the board.

Success!

Ashton Irwin says the band will truly know they've "made it," when folks from their hometown give them a shout-out.

"When someone at the local shopping center says 'Nice song,' that will be the sign because no one from where we are from will compliment you," Ash told www.news.com.au in May 2014.

Ashton Fletcher Irwin was born July 7, 1994, in Hornsby, a suburb on the Upper North Shore of Sydney, Australia. He joined 5 Seconds of Summer in December 2011, after his pal Michael Clifford reached out to him via Facebook; 5 SOS had booked its first gig and, anticipating an audience to be around 200, they realized they needed a drummer.

"Michael sort of over-exaggerated," Ashton recalled during an April 2014 interview with *USA Today*. Only about a dozen people showed up for that first show, but Ash says it remains his favorite performance to date because

The Ashton Lowdown

Full name: Ashton Fletcher Irwin

Birthdate: July 7, 1994

Astrological sign: Cancer

Family: Mom is Anne Marie; siblings are Harry and Lauren

5 SOS role: Drummer

Rep: He's the kind-hearted, chirpy fellow with the really big laugh.

Favorite food: Spaghetti

Favorite singer: English singer-songwriter James Morrison

Favorite album: Trey Songz's *Chapter V*

Favorite TV show: *Family Guy*

Celebrity crush: Paramore's Hayley Williams and actress Mila Kunis

Doppelganger: One Direction's Harry Styles

On Twitter: @Ashton5SOS

Twitter followers: 2.2 million

Random fact

Ashton has a strange fascination with *Today Show Australia* presenter Karl Stefanovic. He's even taken to sending the newscaster tweets, like this one from June 2014: @karlstefanovic you are looking terrific this morning Carl ;)

"it was so new to us. It was a terrible gig, but there was just something about it that me and the boys loved. We knew it was the start of something cool for us."

The guys weren't in show business long before they came to understand firsthand that being in the spotlight means you're subjecting yourself to lots of criticism – sometimes very, very unkind criticism. In April

Rocking the Bandana

One of Ashton's Irwin's most consistent fashion statements is the bandana. Whether it's red, black, gray or green, the bandana is generally folded so that it's about two inches wide and then tied around his head to keep his luscious locks semi-controlled.

Of course, Ash isn't the only musician with a closet full of bandanas. Poison lead singer Brett Michaels loves the bandana, as does One Direction's Harry Styles. And don't forget country legend Willie Nelson. He's worn red bandanas longer than all the rest of the guys have been alive.

Ashton's Tweets

Drummer Ashton Irwin is a fun-loving guy who's not afraid to show a little love for his family and friends. His personality shines through in his tweets, where he often talks about his mom and siblings, his gratitude for 5 SOS' new fame, and, of course, the rest of his band mates. Here's a sampling:

Been so good to have my mum over here in London for a bit :) x. June 10, 2014

Just played Wembley Stadium, it isn't hard to find a 5SOS fan when they are holding the "angry banana" lol. June 6, 2014

Narrow minded articles about us really piss me off, some people just don't listen, we are trying to do something different. June 5, 2014

Seeing 5 Seconds of Summer shirts makes me SO happy man. June 3, 2014

I wonder what woulda happened if I never learnt the drums. May 26, 2014

Musicians putting other musicians down is so lame man, lift each other up, support creativity. May 21, 2014

How me and the boys got to this point amazes me, thanks for giving us the chance to play music around the world. May 15, 2014

Had an amazing two days off with my family, missed them lots and lots :) May 13, 2014

Can't believe people pick on my sister at school, one day they will realize individuality is a beautiful thing, I love you Lauren, be tough. May 1, 2014

To just make someone else happy, with something as simple as playing drums and guitars, is the best thing ever. April 30, 2014

Me and mum just killed a GIANT spider with a deodorant can and a lighter, AUSTRALIA. April 28, 2014

SO homesick. April 15, 2014

Paris is amazing, the fans are incredible, couldn't ask for anything more, love you x. April 2, 2014

Young and free, punk and pretty. March 29, 2014

In my underwear listening to 80's classics. March 14, 2014

When you come to a 5SOS show, I genuinely want you to have possibly one of the best nights of ya life, love you x. Feb. 27, 2014

Ready to tour 😘. Feb. 18, 2014

My new book "Survival Cooking" with Ashton Irwin, to help you survive in a house of teenage males who can only boil/microwave things. Feb. 9, 2014

2014, Ash took to Twitter to defend the band: "Be with us, or against us, don't like what we are doing, it's fine, this is the real s**t, all for the fans, don't dare tell me otherwise."

Within minutes, some spiteful hashtags (#ashtonyourenotgoodenough, for instance) started circulating. Fortunately, fans came to his defense. As for Ash, he dug deep and posted this quote on Twitter: "A heart that hurts is a heart that works." Then, later that same day, he shared a photo of himself onstage with Luke Hemmings, along with the comment: "Love this guy, so happy to be playing shows again, and being behind my drums, X"

5 Seconds of Summer has a love-hate relationship with Twitter and Ashton is the first to admit that it and other social networking outlets have helped the band far more than it has hurt them.

"**You can build a fan base now before you've actually released anything, so it's all quite weird. Whereas before we'd be touring our butts off for like years, but that's not the only way that you can build a fan base which is nice.**"

"I think it's reversed the music industry in a way," he told the website musictakeabow.com in spring 2014. "You can build a fan base now before you've actually released anything, so it's all quite weird. Whereas before we'd be touring our butts off for like years, but that's not the only way that you can build a fan base which is nice."

And build a fan base they have. The days of poorly attended gigs are far behind them and now Ash and his pals find themselves touring the globe, both as headliners and as the opening act for One Direction's 2014 world tour. With a basic understanding and appreciation of cultural differences, the guys are trying hard to please all their fans wherever they live – the States, Australia, Japan, Spain – by creating special versions of their new album that will include some of the songs that didn't make the cut for the debut's first edition.

"It's becoming a lot to think about," Ash told news.com.au in

Only Ashton

Ashton Irwin's popularity is soaring – and so, it seems, is the popularity of his name.

As a boy's name, Ashton is currently the 124th most commonly used name in the United States and the 78th most popular name in Australia. Which got us thinking: Who are some other famous Ashtons?

American actor and producer **Ashton Kutcher** is probably the most recognizable guy to share the name. He first gained fame for his role in TV's *That '70s Show* and now stars in *Two and a Half Men*. Kutcher is also known for his roles in movies including *Jobs*, *Dude, Where's My Car?*, *Just Married*, *The Butterfly Effect*, *The Guardian* and *What Happens in Vegas*. Kutcher's real first name is Christopher; Ashton is his middle name.

Ashton Holmes is an American actor best known for his roles in *A History of Violence*, the HBO miniseries *The Pacific*, CW's *Nikita* and the ABC drama series *Revenge*. Holmes made his debut on television with a recurring role in the soap opera *One Life to Live*.

California-born **Ashton Moio** is an actor, stunt actor and martial artist in film and television. He's best known for playing Rico on the ABC Family show *Twisted*.

What about athletic Ashtons? Australian Cricketers **Ashton Turner** and **Ashton Agar** are both contracted to the Perth Scorchers. **Ashton Sims** is an Australian professional rugby league footballer for the North Queensland Cowboys. And **Ashton Eaton** is an American decathlete and Olympic champion, who holds the world record in both the decathlon and heptathlon events.

Of course, not all Ashton's are male. **Ashton Shepherd** is an American country music singer and songwriter. Her 2008 debut album, *Sounds So Good*, produced two Top 40 hits. In 2011, she released her second album, *Where Country Grows*, which includes the Top 20 hit "Look It Up."

May 2014. "We are trying to do this in three or four continents, and it's intense trying to stay on top of it all."

The songs themselves mean a great deal to the 5 SOS guys and they've set themselves apart from other groups by actually writing their own tunes. The lyrics, they say, reflect their own life experiences and help them connect to the audience in a way they couldn't if they were singing someone else's songs.

"I think that a lot of the songs are quite deep at times; we've been through a lot of stuff," Ash told musictakeabow.com. "A lot has happened to us in the past few years. We've been lonely, we've been happy, we've been sad. A lot has happened and if you really listen closely to the EP and the album that's coming out, it's real stuff that has sort of happened to us."

As they continue to distinguish themselves from musical acts past and present, the guys find themselves educating both fans and music critics about the qualities of rock bands vs. boy bands.

"Someone said to me the other day when they came to see our show, they were like, it's amazing to see people going crazy for some people with guitars on stage, and they said they hadn't seen that in about 10 years. It's nice to see people realize we're trying to do something different. It's really cool," Ashton told the American TV show *Extra*.

"When people say 'Oh, you guys play your instruments', they go 'That's really weird.' It's weird to us because we thought that's just what you do. People listen to our songs and say, 'Did you play on this?' What do you mean? Yeah, it's our song." ★

The Beat Goes On

No doubt about it, Ashton Irwin is a technically proficient drummer with inventive licks and impressive speed. He's the heart of 5 Seconds of Summer — pumping energy and beats into their hit songs.

So, you know about Ashton ... but what do you know about other rock drummers? Can you match the drummer to the band they're best known for performing with?

1. Ringo Starr
2. Phil Collins
3. Keith Moon
4. Charlie Watts
5. John Bonham
6. Keith Harris
7. Rian Dawson
8. Neil Peart
9. Joey Jordison
10. Lars Ulrich

A. Black Eyed Peas
B. The Who
C. The Beatles
D. All Time Low
E. Metallica
F. Rush
G. Slipknot
H. Genesis
I. Rolling Stones
J. Led Zeppelin

Answers: 1-C, 2-H, 3-B, 4-I, 5-J, 6-A, 7-D, 8-F, 9-G, 10-E

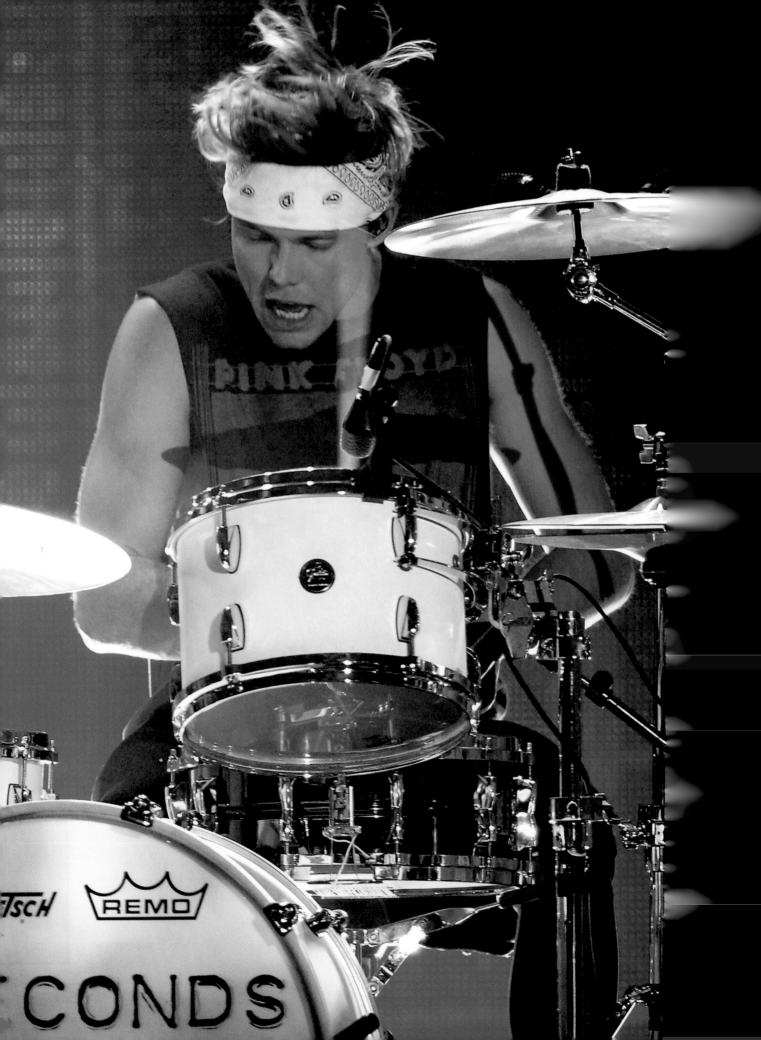

CHAPTER 7

The Future Is Bright

The boys of 5 Seconds of Summer are having a breakout year – and they show no signs of slowing down any time soon. Within the first six months of 2014, they'd already chalked up accomplishments including:

- Reaching the No. 1 sales position in 39 countries within two days of listing their worldwide debut single, "She Looks So Perfect," for pre-order on iTunes.

- Selling out their first North American headlining tour in less than five minutes.

- Becoming the first Australian band in 14 years to score a No. 1 single in the United Kingdom.

- Debuting at No. 2 on the Billboard 200 with their EP *She Looks So Perfect*, nearly overtaking the ultra-popular *Frozen* soundtrack.

- Reconnecting with One Direction to open for that band's *Where We Are* tour in the United States, Canada and Europe.

- Performing live at the Billboard Music Awards in Las Vegas.

- Releasing their self-titled debut album in Europe and Australia – with other releases scheduled throughout the summer.

No surprise then, that music critics and entertainment writers have jumped

onto the 5 Seconds of Summer bandwagon with proclamations such as "5 Seconds of Summer: Like One Direction, But Better" (*The Metro – UK*) and "Next in line for the teen heartthrob throne is 5 Seconds of Summer, four Australian lads with perfectly coiffed hair who appear headed for One Direction levels of success" (*USA Today*). MTV News boldly stated: "Individually, each of the guys is a force to be reckoned with, but together, duh, they're unstoppable" and LA's "The Hot Hits" alerted music fans that 5 SOS is "the band you should be obsessing over."

While all that praise is nice, it's the sort of commentary that has fans slapping their foreheads and saying, "Where have you been for the past few years?"

Yes, 5 SOS is relatively new to the U.S. music scene, but they're not complete rookies at this performing thing. They've already been writing and performing for a couple years and, with minimal marketing, their first music release, an EP titled *Unplugged*,

5 Seconds of Summer
2014 Tour Dates

Feb. 23, 2014	O2 ABC, Glasgow, UK
Feb. 24, 2014	Leadmill, Sheffield, UK
Feb. 25, 2014	The Ritz, Manchester, UK
Feb. 27, 2014	Norwich Nich Rayns LCR UEA, Norwich, UK
Feb. 28, 2014	O2 Academy Oxford, UK
March 2, 2014	The Institute, Birmingham, UK
March 3, 2014	O2 Shepherds Bush Empire, London
March 4, 2014	O2 Shepherds Bush Empire, London
April 11, 2014	Fillmore, San Francisco
April 12, 2014	Wiltern Theatre, Los Angeles
April 15, 2014	House of Blues Dallas, Dallas
April 17, 2014	Riviera Theatre, Chicago
April 18, 2014	Royal Oak Music Theater, Royal Oak, Mich.
April 19, 2014	Sound Academy, Toronto
April 21, 2014	The Fillmore Silver Spring, Silver Spring, Md.
April 22, 2014	Best Buy Theatre, New York, N.Y.
April 24, 2014	Tower Theatre, Upper Darby, Penn.
April 25, 2014	Toyota Oakdale Theatre, Wallingford, Conn.
April 30, 2014	The Enmore Theatre, Sydney, Australia
May 2, 2014	Thebarton Theatre, Adelaide, Australia
May 3, 2014	Palais Theatre, Melbourne, Australia
May 4, 2014	Palais Theatre, Melbourne, Australia
May 5, 2014	The Enmore Theatre, Sydney, Australia
May 7, 2014	The Trivoli, Brisbane Qld, Australia
May 8, 2014	Riverside Theatre, Perth, Australia
May 18, 2014	Billboard Music Awards, Las Vegas
May 23, 2014	Croke Park, Dublin, Ireland (with 1D)
May 24, 2014	Croke Park, Dublin, Ireland (with 1D)
May 25, 2014	Croke Park, Dublin, Ireland (with 1D)
May 28, 2014	Stadium Of Light, Sunderland, UK (with 1D)
May 30, 2014	Etihad Stadium, Manchester, UK (with 1D)
May 31, 2014	Etihad Stadium, Manchester, UK (with 1D)
June 1, 2014	Etihad Stadium, Manchester, UK (with 1D)
June 3, 2014	Murrayfield Stadium, Edinburgh, UK (with 1D)
June 6, 2014	Wembley Stadium, London (with 1D)
June 7, 2014	Wembley Stadium, London (with 1D)
June 8, 2014	Wembley Stadium, London (with 1D)
June 13, 2014	Friends Arena, Järva, Sweden (with 1D)
June 14, 2014	Friends Arena, Järva, Sweden (with 1D)

June 21, 2014	Capital FM Summertime Ball, London (with 1D)
June 24, 2014	Amsterdam Stadium, Amsterdam, The Netherlands (with 1D)
June 25, 2014	Amsterdam Stadium, Amsterdam, The Netherlands (with 1D)
June 28, 2014	San Siro, Milan, Italy (with 1D)
June 29, 2014	Stadio San Siro, Milan, Italy (with 1D)
July 1, 2014	HMV Oxford St., London (5SOS acoustic show)
July 2, 2014	Esprit Arena, Dusseldorf, Germany (with 1D)
July 6, 2014	Stadio Olimpico Di Torino, Turin, Italy (with 1D)
July 8, 2014	Estadi Olimpic Lluis Companys, Barcelona, Spain (with 1D)
July 10, 2014	Estadi Vincente Calderon, Madrid, Spain (with 1D)
July 11, 2014	Estadi Vincente Calderon, Madrid, Spain (with 1D)
July 18, 2014	Hallum FM Summer Live, Sheffield, UK
Aug. 1, 2014	Rogers Centre, Toronto (with 1D)
Aug. 2, 2014	Rogers Centre, Toronto (with 1D)
Aug. 4, 2014	MetLife Stadium, East Rutherford, N.J. (with 1D)
Aug. 5, 2014	MetLife Stadium, East Rutherford, N.J. (with 1D)
Aug. 7, 2014	Gillette Stadium, Foxboro, Mass. (with 1D)
Aug. 8, 2014	Gillette Stadium, Foxboro, Mass. (with 1D)
Aug. 9, 2014	Gillette Stadium, Foxboro, Mass. (with 1D)
Aug. 11, 2014	Nationals Park, Washington, D.C. (with 1D)
Aug. 13, 2014	Lincoln Financial Field, Philadelphia (with 1D)
Aug. 14, 2014	Lincoln Financial Field, Philadelphia (with 1D)
Aug. 16, 2014	Ford Field, Detroit (with 1D)
Aug. 17, 2014	Ford Field, Detroit (with 1D)
Aug. 19, 2014	LP Field, Nashville, Tenn. (with 1D)
Aug. 22, 2014	Reliant Stadium, Houston (with 1D)
Aug. 24, 2014	AT&T Stadium, Dallas (with 1D)
Aug. 27, 2014	Edward Jones Dome, St. Louis (with 1D)
Aug. 29, 2014	Soldier Field, Chicago (with 1D)
Aug. 30, 2014	Soldier Field, Chicago (with 1D)
Sept. 11, 2014	Rose Bowl, Pasadena, Calif. (with 1D)
Sept. 12, 2014	Rose Bowl, Pasadena, Calif. (with 1D)
Sept. 13, 2014	Rose Bowl, Pasadena, Calif. (with 1D)
Sept. 16, 2014	University of Phoenix Stadium, Phoenix (with 1D)
Sept. 19, 2014	Sun Bowl Stadium, El Paso, Texas (with 1D)
Sept. 21, 2014	Alamodome, San Antonio, Texas (with 1D)
Sept. 23, 2014	BOK Center, Tulsa, Okla. (with 1D)
Sept. 25, 2014	Mercedes-Benz Superdome, New Orleans
Sept. 27, 2014	PNC Music Pavilion, Charlotte, N.C.
Sept. 28, 2014	PNC Music Pavilion, Charlotte, N.C.
Oct. 1, 2014	Georgia Dome, Atlanta
Oct. 3, 2014	Raymond James Stadium, Tampa, Fla.
Oct. 5, 2014	Sun Life Stadium, Miami, Fla.
Oct. 8, 2014	Teatro Metropolitan, Mexico City
Oct. 9, 2014	Teatro Metropolitan, Mexico City

reached No. 3 on the iTunes chart in Australia and broke into the Top 20 in both New Zealand and Sweden. They've also been schooled in the workings of a worldwide tour, thanks to their gig as an opening act on One Direction's 2013 *Take Me Home* tour.

The four-piece's 2014 touring schedule is intense, with more than 80 headline and supporting dates. That's the sort of frenzy that may not allow for them to spend much time writing and recording new music. Some bands are able to create on the road, others find the distractions are too much competition.

If the guys' debut album is the hit many critics expect it to be and if they have to wait until October to get back into the studio, it's still likely they'll be able to release another album by mid-2015. It is that strike-while-the-iron-is-hot philosophy that has helped their tour mates, One Direction, debut atop the Billboard 200 with their first three albums.

Miles Raymer covers rock music for the (Chicago) *Reader.* He says

5 Seconds of Summer has set itself apart from the rest by producing music that's played on a standard guitar-bass-drums setup.

"There are no synthesizers, nods to rap music, quasi-folky old-timey imagery, or any of the other gimmicks that other rock groups have relied on to catch the mainstream's attention recently," he wrote, noting that "'She Looks So Perfect's' unfussy structure and amped-up hooks should appeal both to the teens and tweens it's marketed toward and long-time fans of pop punk. In many ways it feels like an artifact from a different time, when hip-hop and dance music were on the fringe and rock was the undisputed dominant sound both aboveground and under."

The critic's viewpoint was encapsulated by a headline that reads: "Like It or Not, 5 Seconds of Summer Is Rock's Future."

Being labeled the "future" of an entire genre of music could be a big burden to bear, but the 5 SOS lads are taking it all in stride, playing the music they want to play and having a blast doing it. What could be better than that? ★

Filling the Trophy Case – Already

The guys have only been playing together for a couple years, but they are already racking up the award nominations – and taking home their share of trophies too.

In 2013, 5 Seconds of Summer won Channel V's Oz Artist Award and MTV's Breakthrough Band Award.

In the first half of 2014, the band was honored by *Kerrang!* magazine as Best International Newcomer. It was a thrill that sent Michael Clifford to Twitter to thank the band's fans: "Honored to win the @wMagazine award for best international newcomer. Thanks all of you for voting your amazing love u guys."

In March 2014, at the Nickelodeon Kids Choice Awards, the boys were named Aussies' Fave Hot New Talent. The band was also nominated for – but didn't win – a half-dozen World Music Awards and a Much Music Video Award.

As this book headed to press, 5 Seconds of Summer had collected nominations for a number of awards that had not yet been announced: three TRL (Italy) Awards, one Teen Choice Award and a whopping eight We Love Pop Awards – including singular nominations for Calum, Ashton, Michael and Luke as "Fittest Boy on the Planet."

Fictional Love from the Fans

Fans show their love for 5 SOS in all sorts of ways. They wear their T-shirts, buy their music, create websites and Tumblr sites … and lots of fans, it seems, have been creating fan fiction dedicated to their musical idols.

Fan fiction – also known as fan fic – is a broadly defined label for stories about characters or settings or celebrities, written by fans. Some fan fic pays tribute to popular fictional characters such as Harry Potter or Twilight's Edward Cullen, while other stories create fictional storylines for real people – like Luke Hemmings, Michael Clifford, Calum Hood and Ashton Irwin. A sampling:

- "Combined" tells the story of five girls and nine guys – The Red Coast, One Direction and 5 Seconds of Summer – traveling the world, performing songs they've written together. The musicians "become close to one another, some closer than others."

- Ashton is a rich, eligible bachelor in "Starting All Over Again." He has no friends and isn't sure he needs one until he gets put in a group with a guy named Luke. Ashton befriends Luke, Luke's friends and his sister, Lily. Ashton and Lily date each other secretly for a while as friends, but when people start to talk, Ashton denies everything. This leads Lily to do things she never thought she'd do …

- In "Don't Stop," 16-year-old Harmony Smith moves from London to Sydney. She doesn't expect to fit in, especially with her rich family and odd looks. Fortunately for her, her first class in her new school is music, where she is taken in by Calum and his friends, Michael, Luke and Ashton.

Works of fan fiction are rarely authorized by the original work's owner, creator, or publisher and often contain a disclaimer stating that the author owns none of the original characters.

Fan fic is almost never professionally published. That's why it became big news in late June 2014, when 25-year-old Anna Todd's stories dedicated to One Direction earned her a six-figure publishing deal. The Texas-born writer's stories about a straight-A student with an obsession for tattooed, pierced "bad boy" Harry Styles have been read more than 800 million times since she first started posting them on the online community Wattpad. Gallery Books offered Todd a publishing contract and there's even talk of a film adaptation down the line.

"I didn't think anything would come of it," she told Sugarscape. "It was just for fun."

To write or read fictional tributes to your four favorite Aussies, check out the fan fic on websites including FanFiction, Archive of Our Own, Wattpad and FicWad.